Time Do Not Stop

Other books by William Guest:

What I Cannot Abandon

Who Are We: Man and Cosmology

Places You Want to Go: Travel Journals

Time Do Not Stop

POEMS BY WILLIAM GUEST

atmosphere press

CONTENTS

for Graham, Jennifer, and Edie Jane

I.

LOVE POEM

When I said one hundred million years
she laughed, slid a casserole into the oven.
Not a laugh of scorn but one of funny.

To change the temperature
of the casserole's molecules, the clusters,
the little galaxies, I drift to rhymes—

luster, bluster, muster—and dimmer
more distant stars. They blend like bands
of bees into one another's space—

stars and eyes and points of light
and lips and nipples and that persisting
question: could it be that streams

of Sagittarius got pulled from its neighborhood
into the crowning halo of our Milky Way?
Honey, she says, will you come to bed?

And why do I say: later—I want to work
on migrating galaxies and their supernovas.
And she says, instead of making love?

She does not care how galaxies are formed
and merge. And Lord knows I have
a peculiar way of living in this world.

THE CANDLE

We camped around the candlelight,
and knew that this was true.
Our backs pressed against the night,
there was nothing we could do.

There were four of us, or five,
certain and calm, in our way.
We watched a candle burn alive,
there was nothing for us to say.

Behind our backs who knew
how much can darkness mask?
A whole universe or two?
No one thought to ask.

The candle burned, an orange pit
alone with tips of bluish white.
All we knew to do was sit
and feel the wonder of the sight.

SERENDIPITY

Two plastic balls in the swimming pool,
about ten inches diameter, one pink, one blue,
toys floating cloud-light on water,
at times touching.

                    Then a breeze whips
from around some corner,
                             and they part:

blue skids fast to the far left,
pink not caught by the breeze.

So it goes – their world, all of it,
floating together while it lasts,
like being is only barely.

They cry out. If they could.

So unannounced a breeze appears, and stops
just as unannounced, as though nothing happened.

The Inadequacy of a Photograph

The job of a photograph
is to grab,

to not allow change,
to grab

a moment in time
as it oozes away, always

disappearing
forever from earth,

to still life
into something

that will no longer
disappear—

at least, its image
will no longer disappear,

as will, ever-changing,
its viewer.

SPRINGTIME

The sky marvels
from where it sits
to see so much green
like when in the 40s

Walt Disney sped up
film to send a flower
from bud to blossom
in presto time,

grass and leaves
faster than yeast,
earth a coloring book
after a hard rain of green.

Thunderstorm

I know I am skin
because the balcony breeze
is wet like a wet breeze feels

lightning sky-cracking

I know I am eyes
because I see light streaks in night
all too brief, again and again

frenetic, sub-atomic brief

I know I am ears
because floods host a chorus
of receding memory

herd-sized bellows roar

I know I am alive
because the squeeze in my heart
is like "You are alive"

alive alive

The Dark

I see my mother pinned on a clothesline,
my father praying with the Mantis.

And I: upside down in a tub of hope.

When my ocean whines I listen;
I ignore the moaning of my sun.

When the egret calls I listen;
I ignore the shaking of the earthquake.

When my lamp bleeds I listen;
I ignore the music of my funeral.

Down the road is a whistle...

If the something I seek is not there to see
I turn my skies to dream.

BROTHERHOOD

Heard the news on TV tonight
that Octavio Paz died.
His life and work were reviewed.
Five minutes.

The "Brotherhood" poem—read by him
at the close of every reading, was read
at the close of him—
is about himself, spelled out, he said,

in the stars...
which is to say (is it not?)
I wish I were writ larger.
So what do they say, all of the poems?

It's not quite right, this experience,
wishing to hug and be hugged
and finding oneself hugging oneself.
Yet I swear to you that in a room

where a few of us are talking
about computers or stocks, I can hear music
coming in, as through a window
through which floats the universe.

A Mystic Visioned Zero

For desert ages
she had sphinxed herself

before the towering lithic honorable numbers—
the ones, twos, and so on—

and thought,
why not? What would appear

if all the ones and twos were to vanish?
A simple circle. It is

the earth, the sun, the round-and-round of days
and years, and lives and lives. Zero.

And oddly, she realized, if you add enough of them
to any number, you see infinity.

When Land is Water

If all of time could be crunched

into a short film we would see

mountains and valleys topsy-turvy

like toys where man or rabbit

would not exist, could not exist.

Continents collide.

Say that again.

Continents collide. Add another film

on another day, show volcanoes

whooping it up to create and destroy,

high and reaching. Don't forget

earthquakes, shaking the jello.

Meanwhile, above, the sky.

The Birth Lottery

Born in my birdbath,
tadpoles, tiny wiggles of life.

Next day they're gone,
all gone—a feast for birds.

I had thought them beautiful,
the tadpoles and the birds.

THE PATRIOT

I'm living such a good life,
a triumph to have been
so sleek and agile. You must know

the joy and thrill of my tongue
snatching an insect, of my skin changing
as I skitter over boundaries of color.

Ah, mating. I cannot say enough
about sex, again and again. At this,
we brown anoles are really good.

Goodbye to the green guys, but we won
the Darwin game. We're conquering
the world, and I'm doing my part.

Just a Little Talk

Tell me God but tell me true

What do you think and what's your view

Is it all right and was it fun

All this work that you've done

Here we are mortals we die so quick

Healthy one day the next day sick

Laugh and joke it's not all bad

Happiness comes to balance the sad

You up there is it all the same

Wonder and worry about the game

What did you want after all

Humans like us on a small blue ball

So you're depressed at how things are

Surely you know having come so far

Looking for meaning? we thought you knew!

!!!!!*@&&$!!!!!!!!!!!!!!!!!!!!!!@*($!!!!

We've been begging for just a clue

The Ideal Man

Let us visualize what makes him so. He's handsome, tall and clever, and is at the right place at the right time to find money, and travels, and social standing. He's the go-to man to turn a trick, to hitch the happening to some might-be event, with an instinct for flashbulbs, and who is standing near.

He goes hunting with the boys, guns and all. Kills the biggest buck, a rack for his mountain lodge. Sings and drinks with pals from high places in the deal-making places.

When charity-giving and galas are the news he's there, to be crowned the one with his coiffured and stunning wife's big eyes glistening.

Known as honest he can be adroit at slight mistruths, turning them into something that seems okay when it's said that way.

I Inherit a Fortune

I lie still, stunned, maybe chilled,
like waking up to nothing, the laughter
in the church when what the preacher said

just came out funny, and the congregation laughed
and the preacher laughed and soon
God laughed and all the angels joined in.

And now, God and angels and preacher and church-goers
and my dead husband and my sons and dead daughter
and all of you everywhere laugh with me.

For the first time in my life I have money.
I am a laughing wealthy woman. The news said straight,
like facts: *Your brother Harry died and left you*

twenty million dollars. I have been poor,
hard working, all of my life. Can you see this?
I am old, at death's door, lying in bed

in a hospital, everybody knows, I know,
I am dying. Maybe a week or two, maybe.
A fight with Harry at 25, and now this, an apology.

Breathe

A pearl diver emerges on the beach
hardly breathing though he needs breath.

The pearl in his hand is a richness unbelieved.
In his hand he holds more than hope.

How beautiful a pearl is. It's nothing
but a pearl, but it's much more than nothing

but a pearl. What riches in this world!
It feels so good to breathe the air.

No more oysters to open, no more ghosts
inside the brain, no more reaching for the sky.

Lone Rider

Poems are opportunities to put something on a plate

Laughing with God

The Meaning of Life

I Inherit a Fortune

Life is

*

It feels so good to breathe,
the pearl in my hand.
What are the riches of this world?
How beautiful it is, this knot.

*

But to the point now. I want to know what and how,

I want to know because I want to know.

*

Time is just a history book

And I am at the tail end of a string of something

WRENS

Look infinity in the face. It's a kitten face.
Hear your child's voice go into the tunnel of your bones.
Hold in your fingers the stem of something.

Next, celebrate the gift that's so brimmed-up full
it is even in the gift that makes you wish
to celebrate the gift. Into this universe you've come, so

when the cold warm winter sun hits where you are sitting
think of no regret and no sorrow. Nothing
in this world can quench the chirping from the nest.

II.

GRAVITY

Newton waking sitting on the side of his bed
Stopped still as a stone frieze
Lost like they say lost in thought
A long time sitting inside the tub of his brain

What is that we could ask Beethoven Einstein
Others whose brains are brains afire
In the wilds of math and art and alchemy
Why can you and I not sit like that

In slow flashes of smoke and mirrors
Strange lands strange stars almost not even there
Where it's found what to name it what is this
Truth lying in wait till someone gets it

Standing up he then walks the Cambridge paths
Saying good morning
Noting that onto this fuzzy earthen ball
He and everything are somehow glued

NEBULA

The stars were just there
when I was a just-there child,
just swarms of tiny tips of light,
motionless fireflies
impaled upon the web of night.

Later they became beacons, sentinels
obeying a secret cosmic drum,
mysterious adornments revealing
the scheme of our world.

Then I saw nuclear furnaces,
countless monolithic cinders of fire
flung from the big bang and still fleeing
while we, a figment of detritus,
grasp the gravity-tail
of an unremarkable one of them.

Other suns, other planets,
other time scales, other beings
to be when other beings are gone?
If I could live on and on and on
I would see stars in some different way.

A Trip to the Store

Distance and speed, tell me this.
How fast is thirty-eight thousand miles per hour?
Six hundred and thirty-three miles with each second's tick.
Voyager I has reached the solar system's edge

crawling along like this for thirty-five years. What is the edge
is unclear: is it the end of solar wind, or
where outside gravity takes over? Is it like a snail on a beach
trying to find the ocean? What would an ant think?

So wonder about this. A man boards a spacecraft,
supplies loaded, enough for a while, and begins his journey
to the edge. He never looks back.
Poor man, what is he doing?

THE REPORT

I'm here to say I've been there, done that,
went traveling throughout the universe,

only a few years for me but for you
more than an earthly lifetime.

I know you're accustomed to your life—
stale, short, quotidian—

a ghost playing boredom games.
I've come back to tell you that we're alone.

My crew and I have searched the universe
and we now have the answer:

we on planet Earth are alone. Yes, my fool,
and to think, there's only one of you.

Nor Any Drop to Drink

Nothing nothing whatsoever more lonely

Than a tiny planet caged into orbit around

One only one of billions of stars inside

One only one of billions of galaxies among

One only one of billions of universes perhaps

A painted ship upon a painted ocean

Anything That Happens Only Once Is Holy

These words, on this page, only once.

Mankind, on this Earth, only once.

The happening of a thing only once, many times.

A bird on a fence, many times.

But *that* bird, on *that* fence, only once.

SOCRATES

Bird in cage, tiger on prowl, mating rabbits,
singing whales, cat with kittens, rose in bloom,
on and on and on and on, and more of the same.

Or something that's chance, wisping into existence,
once not, now gone. Monarch butterfly,
busy beautiful bees, with a fatal virus in the hives.

90% wipe-out 250 million years ago,
70% wipe-out 65 million years ago

Knowing with unknown certainty that another one
is happening now – some kind, some time,
is it coming for us? Do we really want to know?

Look. The sunset is red and orange.
I offered a man in his extreme moment of grieving,
here, take this cup of hemlock, and he said no.

Work in Progress

All that you've done, perfect
was your aim, universe,
and I've seen how well
you've created masterpieces,
stars and trees and mountains
in cornucopious splendor.

But in that stream of space
I had a moment float by
to stand next to a father
clutching in his arms his child,
the result it seemed
of something awry at birth.

A Messy Place

God, God, God, God, God.
All this stuff strewn about
when it was clean here before.

A bang—it was a big one—
how many others have you done?
Did you enjoy this thing you did?

Planets, we are here on one,
caged on earth, no why or what.
We just dance or sing or slave.

We're a blip perhaps to you, and
nothing was wrong with nothing.
Why start this thing, the universe?

How are you to clean this up?
"Nothing again" I hear you say.
Oh, God, how could you?

FOLLOW THE INSTRUCTIONS

1. Write your full name.

[use as many pages as needed.]

2. Who are you?

[take your time; do not complete in less than one lifetime; carry on for as long as there are memories of you, longer if you leave anything that outlasts even them.]

3. What do you want?

[optional.]

Time Do Not Stop

If time stopped
everything would stop. Because

when light does not move
nothing new reaches the eyes

and thunder stands still
between the heavens and trees

and thoughts in mid-formation
suspend, the child just born

cannot give her cry
and the old man at death's door

must stop before his last step.
So we pray to you,

    O Holy Murderous Time,

who speeds us on to oblivion,
keep up the good work.

Why I Am Not a Painter

Fighting through the here and now,
the obvious, that which time and space—

the small dot of time and space—
impose on the natural event of being,
a painter strikes and strokes and hopes.

Give me it, give me something down deep,
give me sight, insight, give me how it is.

How to paint a soul when souls do not exist?
How to grab the fleeting with a dab of oil?
How to spare immortality from death?

Give me it, give me something down deep,
give me sight, insight, give me how it is.

ANOTHER GUINNESS

I am going to describe to you
something that is ineffable
therefore my effort will not succeed
but you may if you are able
take up the task
of understanding what an idea is.

It is an arousal in the brain
of electrical and chemical processes
which altogether
hang out there
like a ghost having power
while being nothing

having use without a reason
having existence and maybe death.
An idea can come and go
stay or die or goad
mystify or satisfy
and yet tell me please what is it?

A Lot of Talk

My dad talks of a man who talks a lot.

He talks about who we are, where did we come from, where are we going.

My dad has some funny friends.

This friend can be seen as funny.

The Caveman, Upon Surveying the Future, Says Meh

I step out of my cave in Southern Europe,
25,000 years ago, and look ahead of me.

There, on the border of France and Switzerland,
is CERN, where theoretical physics is tested.

Huge expense, a city unto itself, machines and facilities
at the stretching edge of our imagination.

At the beginning, a tiny pea had begun to expand,
an explosion, and all of matter and energy

burst out of this seed, particles, quantum fields,
stars and flowers and little human beings.

We don't know why. And never will.
So I go back into my cave.

Full Moon

1.

Keep saying it: it is nothing

2.

A bright silver light
dabbed onto blue,
nothing but hanging stillness

3.

Light in an ocean of night

4.

But no, not this screaming bright

[that full moon is too full]

5.

Moonlight should be harmless

[quiet]

6.

My knees are weak,
I murmur but cannot speak

7.

For sipping slowly
pour a little moonlight
into my teacup

8.

But that's not what's happening
                                    [this light is not for sipping]

9.

[This light is not light]

10.

It's holding me up and tearing me down,
embracing me while letting me drown

III.

Nothing Pines for Something

There's a man who comes from nothing –
not made of flesh and bone like you and me

but of silences, dreams, gravity and lost wax.

He is by nature a music maker,
because music too comes from nothing.

He can draw, paint, sing and dance –
they too come from nothing.

His imagination is the greatest nothing of all.

But his heart pines for something, and his soul
is afraid something does not exist.

THIS ANIMAL

As the plane went down to its crash
I heard a baby crying out, lamenting
that it would not live, after all
it went through just to get here.

*

After 76 years it's come to cancer,
the kind that snuffs out being.
I don't know which is harder to grasp:
being or not being.

*

Immortality. Would I want it?
Death when it happens happens forever,
becomes nothing forever, the nothing
that's nothing, the forever forever.

*

This living is also called being:
this animal that sits atop my heart
with eyes that never blink. And then
it smiles, and gives a knowing wink.

LOVE, YOU ARE TOO MUCH

Each part in nature has a limit. Somewhere there's an end, a precipice.

A few times I have felt it close, looked over at the gloom. So now I will pull back, and later just feel the ache, the ache.

That is when the heart recovers. By stopping short of the otherwise.

*

Love is not love if it does not make you want the night to come.

*

Grieving again through what might have been is useless but how to stop.

The universe might have wobbled, might have spawned a different place, might have been more flower-like.

But I keep feeling the tiny tug of that little black hole in my heart where her face might have been.

THE REST IS MISSING

A
Boy
Can
Date
Every
Friendly
Girl
Half
Inspired
Just
Knowing
Love
May
Not

How to Believe in Ghosts

At age six, outside
my window
a crouching fog
blends trees into wisps.

It is a ghost,
an almost balanced stillness,
the world almost
not breathing.

I want to feel
its face on mine.
I want to hug it, a ghost
hugging a ghost.

This fog is not
just a cloud
nestling on the ground.
It is a lump in my throat.

All My Brothers and Sisters

are gnawing on a bone—
one sister begins her singing,
the rest of us start listening,
then slowly sing her song:

A bee's a beauty bundle
bumbling in the blue
and all the tales we tumble
are bites of gospel true—

the wooded path is merry
with sunshine blotches peeking,
the birds are chirping cheery
in their game of hide and seeking—

stars seem so humble
and pour out wishes lightly,
a moth can only wonder
why light is always shining.

The world is full of fate
where lightning finds its rod.
So, hurry up, don't be late:
we'll glide to the throne of God.

THERE

My brother

wanted me there

when he died.

So I was.

But we wondered

where is there.

HYMN

I've thought about it.

No family left living, siblings gone, at the end being alone, leaving me.

The one who lived the longest.

The last.

It's almost here.

So where is home?

It had always been the place they were.

Soon there will be no one to go to, to grow from.

Oh, too bad it's not true we'll all get together in the sky, Lord, in the sky.

THE LAST SPOON

I wandered on a hazel day
across the lilies of grass
with my father along
the graveyard rows of graves.

O Holy Sun, spray down your light.
I deliver to thee at dusk
this grave-filler.

*

Others have gone
so many times
leaving us, the survivors

watching over what has been,
hardened as tombstones,
granite.

*

At the top of the stairs

huffing and puffing,

legs feeling weak.

Why won't my body into perpetuity
carry on?

*

Here and now, my wrinkles
wrinkle up my face. Have I looked

in the mirror lately? My wife died,
everyone I know has died

or will soon, as I spoon
my grave down to one last spoon.

LIGHTS OUT

The thing about this full moon
is that it is the last at perigee
for me to see

in stricken awe. I don't stumble
but feel I should, to mark
this moment's jolt,

a face in the wispy clouds
so silver, then glowing
only softly, whispering to me

there will be no more.
It happens again
in 20 years, but you are 94.

STILLNESS

Here beside me is my mother
who is 94 and hardly able

to chew her food.

Yet there, in that photo, is my mother,
a 14-year-old

beautiful girl.

I adjust my mind. That was then.
That was she. This is she

as I feed her another bite.

While she changes, everything changes,
like a flower. Except

that girl of 14.

AND I DID

~ for Amy

Quietly I died; it did not hurt.
I knew what I was doing.
I knew an end when I saw one.
I knew how to stop, how to die.

Ghosts floated about my bed,
trying vainly to feed me, give me liquids –
words that I knew sort of fading,
saying to me *this is sad, my dear.*

But I clenched my body shut:
going out of business, everything must go –
give me a moment and I will not be.
You cannot dissuade me.

Sad, yes, hard, no; a final something I had to do.
Its time had come, had come to me.
Beautiful life, I gave it a silent kiss,
and I dared me to take that step, and I did.

METAPHYSICS

I'll go forth to meet my Maker

said my father to the Quaker.

Who's your Maker asked the Quaker.

I'm the salt and He's the shaker;

I'm the bread and He's the baker.

CRY

At first a feeling
    (Webster's: *feeling:* An emotional state or reaction)
then the beginning of a tear
    (Webster's: *tear:* A drop of clear saline fluid secreted by
    the lacrimal gland and diffused between the eye and
    eyelids to moisten the parts and facilitate their motion)

because a memory
    (Webster's: *memory:* the ability and process of the
    brain to recall an experience or activity)

happens only nowhere but the brain
    (Webster's: *brain:* the portion of the vertebrate central
    nervous system...made up of neurons...enclosed
    within the skull)

when within the brain a tear
is caused by a memory, felt—

The Kiss

I see two oceans blue
clear through

and stars
sparkling there

as I lean over and feel
our lips collide.

A Girl and Chance

Much to my last night's unsettlement and happiness
I her elder by many years went to the symphony

with my niece beautiful in ways that youth and beauty
conspire to glow. We sat side by side in the half light

of Beethoven's violin concerto having discussed
over wine and dinner her thoughts of school and life.

She an atom in a river that can smell the salt of the sea
we even talked about how miniscule is a human life.

While I looked at her, a human life not possible to dream,
I wished for her *go forth through your rushing years,*

but birth to death, what is to happen to a girl
whose golden, unguaranteed life is like dice?

FORGOT THE FUTURE

I will forgot tomorrow's
memories of what has yet won't be

across boundaries of now
bumbling up a mind not made—

a want precedes a wish to unknow
the known, feeling tomorrow

in yesterday's recall. Oh
future, how you've been already!

THE DREAM

> *In my dream I have cancer I am poor I am in pain*

Where is the music

> *In my dream I wander mindlessly*

Where are my friends

> *In my dream it's over*

Where is the flower

> *I remember*

> > so much song and light and nectar

HELP

I could not help it

Could not

Help

Could

Not help

Could I

Help

It

I

Could

Poor Man, Rich Man

I hum my tune and have no words.
I have my words and hum no tune.

My eyes have vision; I know this.
Sometimes my words are like moths;

I know this. I am poor.
Inside a warehouse of words

I look and look. In the dark
I fall down and bruise my knee.

I sit with my pencil and pad.
Through my pencil words come

like light. It makes no sense
that I am rich again. But I am rich again.

IV.

Two Lazy Mules

Two lazy mules
hitched to a wooden wagon
haul two boys for a while
whiling away their journey-chore
at the pace of a Georgia dandelion
drifting in a still world:

Frank says, "It's better this way, isn't it?"
Who has barely ever seen a car,
which would not do well on this wagon-rutted road.

He can only imagine it but says,
"Someday when we are speeding along paved highways
inside a metal box, we will not gaze
at the grainy color of the ground alive
with road-side plants, dragonflies
with wings so gossamer there is no word for them…"

70 years later, Frank, lying in his final wagon-bed,
gazing back on all that has occurred,
slow-breathing the same air that holds
Mozart sounds
as lilt as dragonfly wings,
listening while the reins are softly drawing
his chore to its end, says

"It was better that way, wasn't it?"

Autobiography via Automobile

1927 T Model Ford: Cranked by hand, a black beauty, owned by Uncle Jim. In 1938 it sat in his sprawling Georgia farm yard, beneath a big old oak, waiting. To drive it along the dirt road, often muddy, insert the crooked crank at the base of the grill, giving it one or sometimes several muscular quick jerking spins, and *eureka!* the motor growls and coughs and finally comes to life. A small boy jumps into the car with wonder.

1932 Model A Ford: My parents'.
1933 Chevrolet sedan: My parents'.

1935 Chevrolet: My parents' first new car, my Dad's pride. How good does it get? One time I, a child, unthinking, caused a door to be broken. Like his wing was broken.

1936 Packard: Bought in 1942. Almost a luxury car, wartime, when no new cars were made. That old transmission kept getting stuck in low. It happened one time at night, about '47, after dropping off my date: wrenches, grease, fumbling under the dash, flashlight in hand, removing the cover of the transmission box to put the gear in its place. Arrrgggghhh.

1935 Oldsmobile: In Colorado, my college summer job in '51, bought my first car, for $50, quite classy-looking, keeping its chin up. The idea was quite simple: to have a cheap drive home to South Carolina. If it breaks down, just sell it. But instead, each breakdown was too small, nickels and dimes. A water pump cost $15; a used tire, $10. The best-laid plan. I sold it to my brother.

1951 TD MG: Bought in '54. Cannot imagine how I afforded this. But, oh what a car. With the look-at-me beauty of the T Model Ford. I was my own mechanic. We became as close

as blood brothers. That car, with its top down, and my girl
at my side. Hoopla.

1949 Ford: Boy, this was an old clunker, just after law school.
Don't ask about the MG.

1951 Mark V Jaguar Saloon Sedan: Now the aristocrat,
sophisticated. Ford had to go. Now I'm a young lawyer,
waiting to have a chauffer someday.

More to come. Pontiac, Audi, Lexus, BMW convertible.

And in 2018, a brand-new Mercedes-Benz SUV, as of last
Wednesday.

Truth be known, I have loved horses all of my life, and still do.
They don't change.

Something Light

The sun sits a tad above the horizon, rising.

No, that was when I was young.

Now I see it setting.

I cannot change the sun.

There will be an ending time, and it will end.

Surely there is a God of life, hidden.

But I tell you, I do not need anybody except myself.

This is not bragging. This is the truth of fact.

Illegal

A robot I'm not. Hands like any other man
to reach inside the truck's bed, lift
a leaf blower, strap it on a shoulder,

survey the yard brown with leaves.
Move the feet. Bend the back. Rake and rake.
Trim the hedge. Sit beside the truck, eating lunch.

Next house, next yard. Reach inside the truck. Blow
the leaves. Mow
the grass. Trim the hedge.

They drop me at my house, each day alike.
The waning sunlight streams in the window.
I eat my food, drink my beer. Then: tomorrow.

Bowerbird and Goat

The bowerbird with his fuzz and sticks,
building, and the goat tied to his pole, chewing.

Neither Darwin nor any preacher
can say why. Nor all of my thinking

through all of my years to now,
nearing the end surely soon,

has brought light to my knowledge,
has brought insight as to *the point*.

Maybe it's only mating, says the bowerbird.
Or, maybe, says the tethered goat, it's bleating.

THE FARM

So many images of animals hang around my screen door.

Infinity begins at the border of perceptibility.

The sunflowers breathe in the breeze.

A poem is another try at the ineffable.

The calf I knew when I was a child I saw slaughtered.

ANIMALS

These people carved up a cow
and ate it.

Small pieces
they fed to their dogs.

They thought themselves kind
and they loved animals.

*

The butterfly collector:
the butterfly's beauty.

The snake wishes for a friend:
the farmer comes with his hoe.

The chicken clucks in the sunshine:
the hand wrings its neck.

*

Yes, mountains and streams
perish. The sun

shines down, the indifferent moon
rises and falls, and kind man

prods the animals
to their last waterholes:

if earth were our horse, we'd ride
until it died.

*

The pride has a new leader.
He greets the cubs by eating them.

WILD HORSES

We've got to get rid of some horses

The helicopter

The horses running literally for their lives

Shot and then drop

Shot and then drop

Shot and then drop

The deer need to be hunted

But to shoot them when they come to the feeder

Who would do that

On TV the mother wolf died of starvation

There were cameramen and biologists watching

And they let her die

They observed what they observed

And they let it happen

This poem is an exercise in how humans behave

THE SAME CLOTH

They were much like
You and me sitting there weaving

In campfire light laughing
Fingers at work on a blanket

*

Cloth found in old Russian earth
Thirty-five thousand years ago woven

From flax but think of that
The early dawn of modern us

*

What is it like now after they've gone
And millions and millions more

To see the cloth we weave
I raise our candle now

LOCK AND KEY

all i remember from the book
with a title in greek
page after page after page
the words in greek characters
running like a marathon
spilled perhaps with persian blood
or who knows but thats my point

it is written there and i cant read it
a book of knowledge
and maybe more
black on white a code in hiding
and i know it says something
im sure it says something
it does i just know it does

NEVERTHELESS

I.

Legions of Caesar's soldiers
wielded swords, drew blood
and horrified
but never
a single poem.

II.

Most people could hold in hand
a poem, continue talking
for a while, then absent-mindedly
lay the poem down,
like a napkin.

III.

Are not all heads alike?
Life's way is to cram itself
into and through
all living things.
Not many graves have poems.

IV.

Behind a mule and plow
parting the gentle earth in rows,
unnoticed by mule and plowman
and the dog lying in the shade,
poetry dances.

THE MEANING OF LIFE

Said the spider to the human:
I know you're going to kill me.
I know because a sudden flash

of world-filled knowing—
not normal for nothing spiders—
has just now sprung upon me.

How ugly I think you look.
Where are your other legs?
Your hairiness, your highness?

Oh, yes, your size is a wonder,
but I have lit on elephants
where I have found some fleas.

When I meet a human—I see
you at the end of my web—
death to all my legs, to every

single hair of me, my eyes
smushed like so much yucky mud.
I was born to be dead.

GUILT

~Hurricane Harvey, August 2017

like everyone but the millions
in Houston
beyond the rooftops I am safe

*

no flights to take me home
this is disaster in absentia
those little raindrops

*

on endless water tv
dayafterdaymoremoremore
floodingdestroying aplace tocry

*

until one day the sun reveals
now staring at us catastrophe
and that's where I'll go

Deep in the Congo

*based upon an episode in the Congo in which
renegade black soldiers herded
a group of white villagers into the village square and
slaughtered them*

Were you the one, deep?
There in the Congo, deep in love
with verdant, twisting humankind?
Were you the one to bathe the babies' faces
beside the black ruins of ancient jungles, beneath
the trees where you pulled
the babies to cover under leaves,
and rubbed wine upon the uncorked faces of mothers?
Were you the one to see them coming, swarm in swarm?
See them swarming in the black of dreams
that moved with stars and trees,
and pray to God,
biting each prayer before
you let it through your teeth:

    NOT SO MUCH SPACE
    NOT SUCH DISTANT STARS
    NOT TREES SO GREEN
    NOT LIFE SO CLEAR

but let, O God, the lives that happen here
be a casual thing, and not so dear.

*

He the gun under jungle sickness, you were the roof
of his claw-infested cave, sky torn down,

you were the roof he shot, he split, he clawed.
He hoped to see the spaces open wide, to rise
to the skies in tommy-gun waves of fury.

Did you see them coming, blade and gun,
driven lost by lust, and did not run? Did you hear
them shout commands as they herded
children into the square? Did you pray
for God to intervene?

And then the soldiers were hunted down and slaughtered.

*

The end is too right. They rage in day and night.
He is killed by him, a quiz upon the face,
thunders in the earth, trees greener in each slant of light...

Deep in the Congo

      Mr. Kurtz, he born.
A tiny, English, moist-skin
breathing pink blob the world
had not yet seen, nor he it.

      Travel now with Kurtz
through playgrounds, schoolrooms—
the old-time England where he
grew up, configured the world, imagining

      ships with romantic sails
driven by destination dreams
of dark Africa where naked humans
dance and chant in fearful nights.

      There Mr. Kurtz the little king quests
into deeper parts of black, into the vine-
clutched souls with starving eyes,
where he ends the share of life he sorely used.

      He says his last pronouncement:
"the horror, the horror." But instead,
he could have said, like a child,
"the thrill, the thrill."

Enfant Terrible

You were the one,
sweetly bathed,
saying protect me,
I'm a holy child.

Some day could you be
hairy-chested, crapulous,
dangling your part
and automatic rifle?

You, with Your Indifferent Rifle, Will Not Stop

It's far too grand and great to disappear
that aria from the heart

but with one simple wave of the wand
it could be gone forever.

It's far too grand and great to disappear
that huge and beautiful city

but with one simple wave of the wand
it could be gone forever.

It's far too grand and great to disappear
that baby trusting in its crib

but with one simple wave of the wand
it could be gone forever.

My Kingdom for a Horse

If I were a horse I would stand
in front of mirror-lakes and preen
or skate four-legged across plains
on Sunday afternoons.

A horse is what God had in mind.

Yes, I also know, if I were a horse
I would grunt before carts and plows,
beneath saddles on which ride
crazy dreams of others.

We are left to die under millions of stars.

But I would also ask the sun and moon
to take a look at me, and my rider.
When we couple up, we are
delirious in this boundless bond.

Then, it seems there's a purpose.

A Little Gnat on the Page

while writing haiku
a little gnat on the page
is writing haiku

PAEAN TO BEDS

A bed is birth
A bed is sleep
A bed is sex
A bed is dreams
A bed is death

Four simple pillars,
a platform
to frame
rest, play, sickness.

O, in the middle of the night
how the mind can thunder!

Egg and Rose Were Talking

Egg and Rose, in their repose,
were talking.

Egg, said Rose, heaven knows
I'm a beauty.
From the beginning of time
if it's beauty sublime
I am the chosen.

Rose, said Egg, your pardon I beg,
this shape of mine
Is simply divine.

In this life, said Rose,
I have a purpose.

In this life, said Egg,
I am the purpose.

And it was sad, to Egg and Rose,
when a fruit fly came by,
to think how short the life
of a tiny thing that can only fly.

CLIMBING A TREE

When you were a boy, you hugged
the limbs, your arms clutching arms,
rough bark on tender skin, arriving
above branches to see below.

How could you know that as a man
you would again climb the trees,
this time with ropes and saws, to seek
not like yesterday

exhilaration in the sky-reaching flower?
This time your intent is to end,
buzz-sawing limb by limb, letting ropes
take them down slow,

one by one from high to low,
taking down this tree until there is no tree.
And, just like that, it's not true
that climbing a tree is climbing a tree.

Down for Good

You will forget me, who used to spread
armsome limbs against the sky,
you sitting on your cushion in the garden,
I who claimed a righteous space aloft and large
so your eyes could sip the green of leaves,
the grey-black bark, the peace for your mind.

You will forget me,
so naked now taken down to trunk and stump.
Who will follow me? A baby tree
to start again where I started 50 years ago,
where I in one solitary forever spot
became peer to pines and oaks,

sheltering birds song after song and squirrels
limb-scampering for nuts through cycles of breeding,
I who was great in any worthy story,
who carried on my work as mighty
among the countless trees, but now, this day,
my race is run: I'm coming down for good.

PENCIL AND PAD

In a room, dark, with some small light,
Sat an old man with pencil and pad.

An old man sat with pencil and pad
In a room without much light.

The room was still and the old man still
And the light was still and the pencil and pad.

The night was quiet and the old man quiet
And silent the light and the pencil and pad.

Time did not move the pencil and pad
In the night and room where the old man sat.

Then the old man laid down
His pencil and pad and turned out the light.

About Atmosphere Press

Atmosphere Press is an independent full-service publisher for books in genres ranging from non-fiction to fiction to poetry, with a special emphasis on being an author-friendly approach to the challenges of getting a book into the world. Learn more about what we do at atmospherepress.com.

We encourage you to check out some of Atmosphere's latest releases, which are available at Amazon.com and via order from your local bookstore:

Adrift, poems by Kristy Peloquin

Ghost Sentence, poems by Mary Flanagan

That Scarlett Bacon, a picture book by Mark Johnson

That Beautiful Season, a novel by Sandra Fox Murphy

What I Cannot Abandon, poems by William Guest

Such a Nice Girl, a novel by Carol St. John

Makani and the Tiki Mikis, a picture book by Kosta Gregory

What Outlives Us, poems by Larry Levy

How Not to Sell, nonfiction by Rashad Daoudi

All the Dead Are Holy, poems by Larry Levy

Winter Park, a novel by Graham Guest

Rescripting the Workplace, nonfiction by Pam Boyd

Surviving Mother, a novella by Gwen Head

Who Are We, a poem by William Guest

ABOUT WILLIAM GUEST

William Guest, the author of *Who Are We, Places You Want to Go*, and *What I Cannot Abandon*, graduated from Yale University in 1953 and Harvard Law School in 1957. A practicing attorney from 1957-1985, he was chair and CEO of a life insurance enterprise engaged in acquisitions from 1985-2006. Writing and sculpting is his third career.

His poems have appeared in venues such as *The New Lantern Review, Calliope, Storyteller Magazine, The Listening Eye*, and three anthologies of Texas Poetry by Mutabilis Press. He was also a juried poet in The Houston Poetry Fest.

Guest is a South Carolina native and long-time resident of Houston, Texas. He is a life member of the Philosophical Society of Texas, the Houston Philosophical Society, and the Board of Visitors of McDonald Observatory, as well as a board member of the Houston chapter of Texas Nature Conservancy, Mercury Baroque Orchestra, and an Advisory Director of Public Poetry.

Learn more at williamguest.com.